Save the Ducks!

by Norma Morales

Illustrated by Peter Church

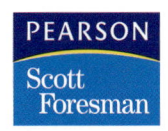

PEARSON
Scott Foresman

Editorial Offices: Glenview, Illinois • Parsippany, New Jersey • New York, New York
Sales Offices: Needham, Massachusetts • Duluth, Georgia • Glenview, Illinois
Coppell, Texas • Sacramento, California • Mesa, Arizona

oil

duck

Oh, no! Oil has spilled into the water. The ducks are in trouble. Their wings are covered with black oil. They cannot fly. They look sick. Did they drink the polluted water?

---

polluted: dirty

volunteers

These volunteers work without pay. They will help the ducks.

Volunteers hurry to the spilled oil. They must help the ducks quickly. It is hard to catch the ducks. The water is choppy. It pounds against the boat. The boat is rolling from side to side. Finally, the volunteers catch all the ducks.

---

choppy: rough, filled with waves

The volunteers take the ducks to a vet. There is more work to do. First the volunteers wipe the ducks with towels. They wipe off as much oil as they can. Then they check the ducks for broken bones or cuts.

---

vet: veterinarian, a doctor for animals

The ducks are sick from drinking the polluted water. The vet gives them medicine. Then the ducks rest in a warm, peaceful place.

The volunteer has learned how to help animals.

towel

The ducks eat some food. They begin to feel better. But they are not healthy yet. Feathers with oil on them are not **waterproof**. The ducks will drown in water if their feathers are still oily. Also, oily feathers cannot keep the ducks warm.

---

waterproof: able to keep out water

The volunteers wash out the rest of the oil with dish soap and warm water. They wash the ducks again and again until all the oil is gone. Then they rinse the soap away. Now they will take the ducks to a new, clean home.

The ducks are healthy. The volunteers take them to clean water. The water is cold, but it will not hurt the ducks. They rush into the water and begin to paddle, swim, and quack.

How do you think the volunteers feel now?